W9-ACR-357

EASY PEN and PAPER TRICKS

beginner magic

Stephanie Turnbull

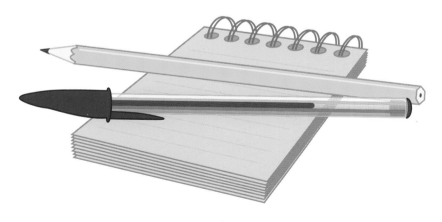

A⁺
Smart Apple Media

Published by Smart Apple Media, an imprint of Black Rabbit Books
P.O. Box 3263, Mankato, Minnesota, 56002
www.blackrabbitbooks.com

Printed in the United States of America, at Corporate Graphics
in North Mankato, Minnesota.

Designed and illustrated by Guy Callaby
Edited by Mary-Jane Wilkins

Library of Congress Cataloging-in-Publication Data

Turnbull, Stephanie.
 Easy pen and paper tricks / Stephanie Turnbull.
    pages cm. -- (Beginner magic)
 Includes index.
 ISBN 978-1-62588-009-3 (library bound)
 1. Magic tricks--Juvenile literature. I. Title.
 GV1548.T863 2014
 793.8--dc23
                                2012051826

Photo acknowledgements
t = top, b = bottom
page 2 iStockphoto/Thinkstock;
4t Dan Kosmayer /Shutterstock.com,
4b Ingvar Bjork/Shutterstock.com;
5 Solomiya Trylovska/Shutterstock.com;
20 Andrey Eremin/Shutterstock.com
Cover images: scissors, hand with pen, red pen,
hat and wand, red curtain all iStockphoto/
Thinkstock, paper scraps Zoonar/Thinkstock

DAD0508b
062014
9 8 7 6 5 4 3 2

Contents

Getting Started

You can do amazing magic with a pen and paper! Make your friends think you're a mind-reader, math genius, or master of illusion—but always practice first.

Math magic

Some pen and paper tricks use calculations that always lead to a certain number. These tricks are called self-working tricks because you don't need to do any secret moves. They're perfect for beginner magicians!

Tips and Ideas

Look out for these boxes as you read this book. They're full of handy tips for making tricks work perfectly.

Sneaky stuff

Other pen and paper tricks may involve clever cutting, tearing, folding, or twisting. In some you pretend to write one thing while really scribbling another.

Magic Secrets

You can also discover the secrets of master magicians in these boxes... but don't tell anyone!

Math Mind-Reader

Start with this quick self-working math trick.

1. Ask your friend to think of a three-digit number in which the first digit is higher than the last and write it down. Don't look!

2. Now ask them to reverse the digits, write them underneath, then subtract the second number from the first.

Give your friend a calculator if they need help with the math!

3. Ask them to reverse the digits of the answer, write them underneath, then add the two numbers. The answer will always be the same: 1089.

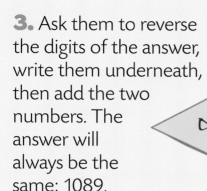

4. Tell them to focus on the number while you read their mind. Pretend to concentrate hard.

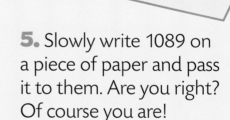

5. Slowly write 1089 on a piece of paper and pass it to them. Are you right? Of course you are!

Magic Secrets

Mind-reading magicians are good actors. They often pretend to be spooky and mysterious.

❄ Magic Dice

This math trick uses two dice. Borrow them from board games!

1. Tell a friend to throw one die on the table. Turn away so you can't see—or do this blindfolded.

2 + 2 = 4
4 + 5 = 9
9 x 5 = 45

2. Ask them to write down the number they threw and double it. Next, ask them to add five... then multiply by five.

3. Now tell them to roll the second die, and add that number to the total.

2 + 2 = 4
4 + 5 = 9
9 x 5 = 45

45 + 5 = 50

4. Ask them what their final number is. In your head, subtract 25 from their answer. You'll get a two-digit number. The first digit is the first number they threw, and the second digit is the second number.

$$50 - 25 = 25$$

Practice taking 25 from different numbers so you can do it quickly.

5. While you work this out, pretend to concentrate on the dice...

I think you threw a two... then a five!

... then tell your friend the numbers they threw!

Magic Secrets

Some magicians flip dice in their fingers so the number of dots seems to change.

What's the Word?

Use a simple math trick to do some really impressive mind-reading!

dog

9

1. Before you perform, choose a book and memorize the first word on page 9. Keep the book nearby.

2. Ask a friend to write down any four digits. Don't look!

7352

3. Now ask them to write the same digits again in a different order, then take away the smaller set from the bigger one.

```
  7352
- 5237
  ────
  2115
```

Magic Secrets

Tricks like this are called book tests. Some are more complicated, but work in a similar way.

4. Ask them to add the four new digits together. If this makes a two-digit number, tell them to add the two digits. They must end up with one digit—which is always 9.

$$7352$$
$$-5237$$
$$\overline{2115}$$

$$2+1+1+5=9$$

5. Look around for a book and pick up the one you chose. Tell your friend to turn to the page matching their number and concentrate on the first word.

6. Stare hard at your friend and pretend to "see" the word... then say the one you memorized.

I'm seeing an animal... bigger than a mouse... not a cat...it's a dog!

If you prefer, write or draw it!

For greater effect, learn words from a few books and let your friend choose one.

Checks and Crosses

Baffle a friend with this torn paper trick.

1. Find a square of thin cardstock or thick paper. Draw a check, a cross, and another check across the top.

2. Draw two more lines of alternating, evenly-spaced checks and crosses.

3. Now tear the paper into nine squares, each with a check or cross.

4. Put them in a small bag and ask your friend to shake them up. Say that you can sense checks and crosses using your magical fingertips.

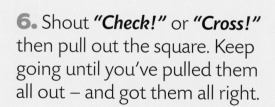

5. Close your eyes then reach into the bag for a square. Hold it inside the bag and quickly feel the edges.

If it has ONE straight, untorn edge, it's a cross.

If it has TWO straight edges, or NONE, it's a check.

6. Shout **"Check!"** or **"Cross!"** then pull out the square. Keep going until you've pulled them all out – and got them all right.

Don't let your friend study the squares afterwards!

13

Can't Copy Me!

Send someone loopy with
this paper loop trick.

1. Cut two strips of
paper, each about three feet (1 m) long. You
may need to tape a few shorter strips together.
Show them to a friend.

2. Join the ends of one
strip to make a big loop
and tape it together.
Give it to your friend.

Ask your
friend to hand
you some tape
or a pen while
you make your
loop, so they don't
notice the twist.

3. Now tape another strip in
a loop for yourself—but sneakily
turn over one end before taping
it, so there's a twist in the paper.

4. Say that you can magically make your paper one-sided and challenge your friend to copy you. Give them a thick pen and ask them to draw a line all along one side of the paper until they get to where they began. Do the same with your loop.

5. Your friend's line will soon be finished, but yours will go on... and on... until you've covered both sides of the paper. Say, ***"See? My loop only has one side!"***

Magic Secrets

Another version of this trick involves cutting along the middle of the loops instead of drawing. Try it and see what happens!

Paper Acrobat

This neat folding trick works best with your friend sitting next to you, not opposite.

1. Draw a person on a rectangle of paper and tell a friend it's an acrobat. Say, *"He gets ready to jump…"*

2. Fold the paper in half lengthways.

3. Now bring the right end across to fold it in half again.

4. Fold it in half again from the right.

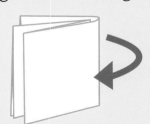

Hold up the paper in front of your friend to show you haven't turned it.

5. Hold the folded paper with your finger and thumb. Say, *"... then he FLIPS over."*

Snap your fingers for effect.

6. Now unfold the first back section to the right.

7. Then unfold the rest of the paper to the left.

8. Open the paper and say, *"Now he's standing on his head!"*

Magic Secrets

Some magicians do this trick with a dollar bill, then make it vanish by hiding it between their fingers.

Impress a group of friends with this trick. Make sure no one can see what you're writing!

You will choose Mrs. Ward

1. Before you perform, write on a piece of paper, **"You will choose..."** and a teacher's name. Seal it in an envelope.

2. Put a notepad, a pen and a hat or box on a table. Give someone the envelope to look after. Don't tell them what it is.

You could name actors, pop stars or TV shows instead of teachers.

Mr. Jackson

Mrs. Ward

Good one... I like him, don't you?

3. Sit back with the notepad and ask people to call out names of teachers at school. Pretend to write each name, but instead put the name from the envelope. Tear off each sheet, fold it and put it in the hat.

Chat to take attention away from the notepad.

You could spell one name wrongly on purpose and throw it away, making sure everyone sees it.

Mrs. Tremaine

Mrs. Wa

Oops, I'll start that again...

4. Keep going until someone has said the name from the envelope and you have more than ten pieces of paper in the hat.

5. Ask someone to take a piece of paper from the hat and read out the name.

6. Say that you made a prediction earlier. Ask your friend to open the envelope. You were right!

Magic Secrets

Magicians often ask people questions to distract them from crafty moves.

You will choose Mrs. Ward

Now saw someone in half...
using a paper person, of course!

1. Before you perform, cut two slits down the front of an envelope, like this. Cut a long piece of cardstock, thin enough to fit through the slits.

2. Ask a friend to draw a person on the cardstock. This will be your assistant!

3. Keeping the envelope face down on the table, seal it with tape and cut off both ends with scissors.

The slits are hidden underneath.

Magic Secrets

Sawing illusions use containers with secret compartments or false bottoms. The saw is usually real!

4. Hold the envelope with the slits facing you. Feed the card in one end, through the first slit, back in the second slit, and out of the other end.

View from underneath

What the audience sees

Your friend should think that the card went straight through the envelope.

Practice gliding the card through the slits.

5. Lay the envelope face down on the table and carefully cut it in half. Pretend to cut everything, but just cut the envelope, not the card underneath.

6. Hold the two halves of the envelope together and slowly pull out the card. Your assistant is whole again. Phew!

Useful Magic Words

book test
A trick in which someone memorizes a word from a book and the magician pretends to read their mind to discover it.

die
A six-sided cube with dots for numbers.

digit
A figure from 0 to 9 that may be part of a bigger number.

illusion
Something that seems impossible.

prediction
Something written or said before it actually happens.

prop
Any object that helps a magician do a trick.

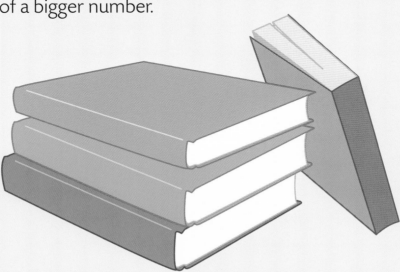

sawing illusion

A trick in which an assistant lies in a box which is sawn in half by a magician. The halves are moved back together and the assistant climbs out, unhurt. There are many versions of this trick.

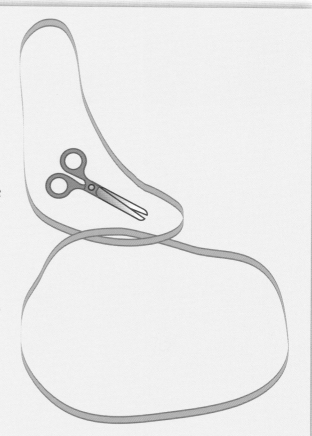

self-working trick

A trick that doesn't need special skills and which works every time, as long as you remember what to do.

Magic Web Sites

To learn more about pen and paper magic and try extra tricks, visit these helpful web sites:

www.sumssimple.com/maths-magic-numbers.html

http://magic.about.com/od/predictions/Easy_Prediction_Tricks.htm

www.boyscouttrail.com/cub-scouts/magic_tricks.asp

🐰 Index

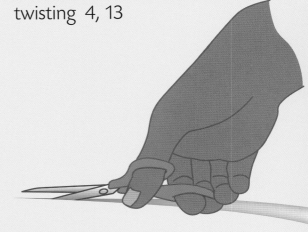